Prayers for My Family

DATE   **NAME**

Be Still and Know That I'm With You...
Psalm 46:10

Prayers for Myself

DATE	REFLECTIONS

Prayers For My Friends

DATE   NAMES

For with God, nothing is impossible...

Prayers For my loves

DATE	NAME

My Prayer

Prayer JOURNAL

PERSONAL REFLECTIONS

Spiritual Inspiration

" I can do All
THINGS
through
CHRIST
WHO STRENGTHENS ME "

- PHILIPPIANS 4:13 -

DATE / /

Sermon JOURNAL

WHAT I LEARNED TODAY

Notes:

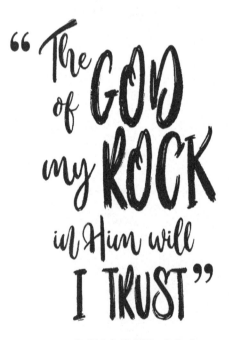

" The of GOD my ROCK in Him will I TRUST "

- 2 SAMUEL 22:3 -

Sermon JOURNAL

WHAT I LEARNED TODAY

Notes:

" I will walk by
FAITH
even when I can't
SEE "

- 2 CORINTHIANS 5:1 -

DATE / /

Sermon JOURNAL

WHAT I LEARNED TODAY

Notes:

" Be Still
in the Presence
of the LORD
and wait patiently
for him to act. "

- PSALM 37:7 -

DATE / /

Sermon JOURNAL

WHAT I LEARNED TODAY

Notes:

" I Praise You
I AM BECAUSE
fearfully and wonderfully
MADE"

- PSALM 134:14 -

DATE / /

Sermon JOURNAL

WHAT I LEARNED TODAY

Notes:

" *Be Not Afraid,* ONLY **BELIEVE** "

- MARK 5:36 -

I AM GRATEFUL FOR

DATE / /

Sermon JOURNAL

WHAT I LEARNED TODAY

Notes:

"By his wounds WE ARE HEALED"

- ISAIAH 53:5 -

I AM GRATEFUL FOR

Prayer Requests

DATE	NAMES

Prayer Card

Prayer Card

Hymn Study

HYMN:

Favorite Verse

Lyrics of Faith

Sing to him, Sing praise to him, tell of all his wonderful acts.
Psalm 105:2

sermon NOTES

DATE / /   **TOPIC:**

SPEAKER: **PLACE OF WORSHIP:**

SCRIPTURE   **NOTES**

Key Points

sermon TRACKER

DATE

SCRIPTURE

NOTES

Reflections

Today's stand-out verse:

I am thankful for:

Prayer Requests:

Inspirational Scripture:

sermon NOTES

DATE / /   **TOPIC**

Scripture

Prayer & Praise

Personal Reflections

sermon NOTES

DATE / /

SERMON

Scripture

Notes

Be on your guard; stand firm in the faith; be courageous; be strong.
1 Corinthians 4:16-18

Sermon NOTES

DATE / /   TOPIC:

SPEAKER: PLACE OF WORSHIP:

Key Points

In GOD we trust

DATE:

This week I will focus on:

What I am most grateful for:

In GOD we trust

DATE:

This week I was most blessed by:

My calling in life is:

In GOD we trust

My favorite passage of scripture is:

God is leading me to make the following changes:

In GOD we trust

DATE:

I feel God's presence most when:

What brings me the most joy is:

In GOD we trust

My spiritual gifts are:

My enthusiasm for the gospel is increased when:

In GOD we trust

DATE:

One way I can apply the gospel to my life is:

An act of obedience God is prompting me to take is:

My time with the LORD

DATE:

Scripture that inspired me today:

Dear Lord:

"Not by My STRENGTH, by His"

~Zechariah 4:6

> " Be Still in the Presence of the LORD and wait patiently for him to act. "
>
> - PSALM 37:7 -

"I will not be SHAKEN"

- PSALM 16:8 -

" FOLLOW YOUR
faith
and he'll lead
THE WAY "

Prayers for My Family

	DATE	NAME
○		
○		
○		
○		
○		
○		
○		
○		
○		
○		
○		
○		
○		
○		
○		

Be Still and Know That I'm With You...

Psalm 46:10

Prayers for Myself

DATE	REFLECTIONS

Prayers For My Friends

DATE	NAMES

For with God, nothing is impossible...

Prayers For my loves

DATE	NAME

My Prayer

Prayer JOURNAL

PERSONAL REFLECTIONS

Spiritual Inspiration

" I can do All THINGS through CHRIST WHO STRENGTHENS ME "

- PHILIPPIANS 4:13 -

WHAT I LEARNED TODAY

Notes:

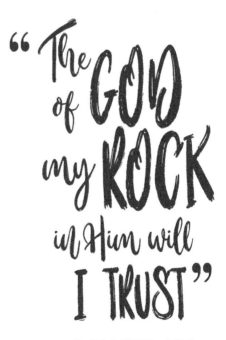

" The GOD of my ROCK in Him will I TRUST "

- 2 SAMUEL 22:3 -

Sermon JOURNAL

WHAT I LEARNED TODAY

Notes:

" I will walk by
FAITH
even when I can't
SEE "

- 2 CORINTHIANS 5:1 -

DATE / /

WHAT I LEARNED TODAY

Notes:

" Be Still
in the Presence
OF THE **LORD**
and wait patiently
for him to act. "

- PSALM 37:7 -

DATE / /

Sermon JOURNAL

WHAT I LEARNED TODAY

Notes:

" I Praise You
I AM BECAUSE
fearfully and wonderfully
MADE "

- PSALM 134:14 -

DATE / /

Sermon JOURNAL

WHAT I LEARNED TODAY

Notes:

"Be Not Afraid,
ONLY BELIEVE"

- MARK 5:36 -

I AM GRATEFUL FOR

DATE / /

Sermon JOURNAL

WHAT I LEARNED TODAY

Notes:

"By his wounds we are **HEALED**"

- ISAIAH 53:5 -

I AM GRATEFUL FOR

Prayer Requests

DATE   NAMES

Prayer Card   Prayer Card

Hymn Study

HYMN:

Favorite Verse

Lyrics of Faith

Sing to him, Sing praise to him, tell of all his wonderful acts.
Psalm 105:2

sermon NOTES

DATE / /   TOPIC:

SPEAKER: PLACE OF WORSHIP:

SCRIPTURE   NOTES

Key Points

sermon TRACKER

DATE

SCRIPTURE

NOTES

Reflections

DATE

Today's stand-out verse:

I am thankful for:

Prayer Requests:

Inspirational Scripture:

sermon NOTES

DATE / /   **TOPIC**

Scripture

Prayer & Praise

Personal Reflections

sermon NOTES

DATE / /

SERMON

Scripture

Notes

Be on your guard; stand firm in the faith; be courageous; be strong.
1 Corinthians 4:16-18

Sermon NOTES

DATE / /   **TOPIC:**

SPEAKER: **PLACE OF WORSHIP:**

Key Points

In GOD we trust

DATE:

This week I will focus on:

What I am most grateful for:

In GOD we trust

DATE:

This week I was most blessed by:

My calling in life is:

In **GOD** *we trust*

DATE:

My favorite passage of scripture is:

God is leading me to make the following changes:

DATE:

I feel God's presence most when:

What brings me the most joy is:

In GOD we trust

DATE:

My spiritual gifts are:

My enthusiasm for the gospel is increased when:

DATE:

One way I can apply the gospel to my life is:

An act of obedience God is prompting me to take is:

My time with the LORD

DATE:

Scripture that inspired me today:

Dear Lord:

"Not by my
STRENGTH,
by His"
-Zechariah 4:6 -

"I will not be SHAKEN"

- PSALM 16:8 -

" FOLLOW YOUR
faith
and he'll lead
THE WAY **"**

Prayers for My Family

DATE   **NAME**

Be Still and Know That I'm With You...
Psalm 46:10

Prayers for Myself

DATE	REFLECTIONS

Prayers For My Friends

DATE	NAMES

For with God, nothing is impossible...

Prayers For my loves

DATE	NAME

My Prayer

Prayer JOURNAL

PERSONAL REFLECTIONS

Spiritual Inspiration

" I can do All THINGS through CHRIST WHO STRENGTHENS ME "

- PHILIPPIANS 4:13 -

DATE / /

Sermon JOURNAL

WHAT I LEARNED TODAY

Notes:

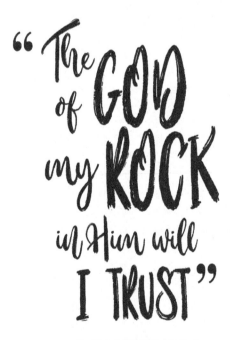

" The of **GOD** my **ROCK** in Him will **I TRUST** "

- 2 SAMUEL 22:3 -

Sermon JOURNAL

WHAT I LEARNED TODAY

Notes:

" I will walk by
FAITH
even when I can't
SEE "

- 2 CORINTHIANS 5:1 -

Sermon JOURNAL

WHAT I LEARNED TODAY

Notes:

" *Be Still*
in the Presence
of the **LORD**
and wait patiently
for him to act. "

- PSALM 37:7 -

Sermon JOURNAL

WHAT I LEARNED TODAY

Notes:

" I Praise You
I AM BECAUSE
fearfully and wonderfully
MADE "

- PSALM 134:14 -

Sermon JOURNAL

WHAT I LEARNED TODAY

Notes:

" Be Not Afraid, ONLY BELIEVE "

- MARK 5:36 -

I AM GRATEFUL FOR

Sermon JOURNAL

DATE / /

Notes:

" By his wounds
WE ARE HEALED "

- ISAIAH 53:5 -

I AM GRATEFUL FOR

Prayer Requests

DATE	NAMES

Prayer Card

Prayer Card

Hymn Study

HYMN:

Favorite Verse

Lyrics of Faith

Sing to him, Sing praise to him, tell of all his wonderful acts.
Psalm 105:2

sermon NOTES

DATE / /   **TOPIC:**

SPEAKER: **PLACE OF WORSHIP:**

SCRIPTURE   **NOTES**

Key Points

sermon TRACKER

DATE

SCRIPTURE

NOTES

Reflections

Today's stand-out verse:

I am thankful for:

Prayer Requests:

Inspirational Scripture:

sermon NOTES

DATE / / TOPIC

Scripture

Prayer & Praise

Personal Reflections

sermon NOTES

DATE / /

SERMON

Scripture

Notes

Be on your guard; stand firm in the faith; be courageous; be strong.
1 Corinthians 4:16-18

Sermon NOTES

DATE / /   **TOPIC:**

SPEAKER: **PLACE OF WORSHIP:**

Key Points

In GOD we trust

DATE:

This week I will focus on:

What I am most grateful for:

In GOD we trust

DATE:

This week I was most blessed by:

My calling in life is:

In GOD we trust

DATE:

My favorite passage of scripture is:

God is leading me to make the following changes:

In GOD we trust

DATE:

I feel God's presence most when:

What brings me the most joy is:

In GOD we trust

DATE:

My spiritual gifts are:

My enthusiasm for the gospel is increased when:

In GOD we trust

DATE:

One way I can apply the gospel to my life is:

An act of obedience God is prompting me to take is:

My time with the LORD

DATE:

Scripture that inspired me today:

Dear Lord:

"Not by my
STRENGTH,
by His"
— Zechariah 4:6 —

" Be Still
in the Presence
OF THE LORD
and wait patiently
for him to act. "

- PSALM 37:7 -

"I will not be SHAKEN"

- PSALM 16:8 -

" FOLLOW YOUR
faith
and he'll lead
THE WAY "

Prayers for My Family

DATE	NAME

Be Still and Know That I'm With You...

Psalm 46:10

Prayers for Myself

DATE   **REFLECTIONS**

Prayers For My Friends

DATE	NAMES

For with God, nothing is impossible...

Prayers For my loves

DATE   NAME

My Prayer

Prayer JOURNAL

PERSONAL REFLECTIONS

Spiritual Inspiration

" I can do All THINGS through CHRIST WHO STRENGTHENS ME "

- PHILIPPIANS 4:13 -

Sermon JOURNAL

WHAT I LEARNED TODAY

Notes:

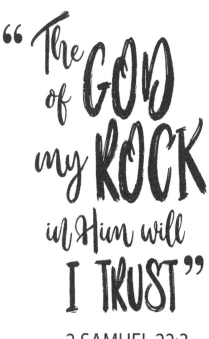

" The GOD of my ROCK in Him will I TRUST "

- 2 SAMUEL 22:3 -

Sermon JOURNAL

WHAT I LEARNED TODAY

Notes:

" I will walk by
FAITH
even when I can't
SEE "

- 2 CORINTHIANS 5:1 -

DATE / /

Sermon JOURNAL

WHAT I LEARNED TODAY

Notes:

" Be Still
in the Presence
of the **LORD**
and wait patiently
for him to act. "

- PSALM 37:7 -

DATE / /

Sermon JOURNAL

WHAT I LEARNED TODAY

Notes:

" I Praise You
I AM BECAUSE
fearfully and wonderfully
MADE "

- PSALM 134:14 -

DATE / /

Sermon JOURNAL

WHAT I LEARNED TODAY

Notes:

" *Be Not Afraid,* ONLY **BELIEVE** "

- MARK 5:36 -

I AM GRATEFUL FOR

DATE / /

Sermon JOURNAL

WHAT I LEARNED TODAY

Notes:

" By his wounds
WE ARE HEALED "
- ISAIAH 53:5 -

I AM GRATEFUL FOR

Prayer Requests

DATE   **NAMES**

Prayer Card   Prayer Card

Hymn Study

HYMN:

Favorite Verse

Lyrics of Faith

Sing to him, Sing praise to him, tell of all his wonderful acts.
Psalm 105:2

sermon NOTES

DATE / /   **TOPIC:**

SPEAKER: **PLACE OF WORSHIP:**

SCRIPTURE   **NOTES**

Key Points

sermon TRACKER

DATE

SCRIPTURE

NOTES

Reflections

Made in the USA
Monee, IL
22 February 2022

91650013R00070